LAURA ASHLEY
COMPLETE GUIDE TO HOME DECORATING